To My
Grandchild
with Love

Susan Polis Schutz

Blue Mountain Press™
Boulder, Colorado

Library of Congress Control Number: 2016940635
ISBN: 978-1-68088-064-9

◪ and Blue Mountain Press are registered in U.S. Patent and Trademark Office.
Certain trademarks are used under license.

Printed in China.
First Printing: 2016

✪ This book is printed on recycled paper.

This book is printed on paper that has been specially produced to be acid free (neutral pH) and contains no groundwood or unbleached pulp. It conforms with the requirements of the American National Standards Institute, Inc., so as to ensure that this book will last and be enjoyed by future generations.

Blue Mountain Arts, Inc.
P.O. Box 4549, Boulder, Colorado 80306

Contents

To My Grandchild
with Love

I looked at you today
and saw the same sensitive eyes
that looked at me with love
when you were a baby
I looked at you today
and saw the same angelic mouth
that made me cry when you
first smiled at me
when you were a baby
It was not long ago
that I held you in my arms
long after you fell asleep
and I just kept rocking you

Every day is exciting
as I continue to watch you grow
I want you to always know that
in good and bad times
and no matter what you do
or how you think
or what you say
you can depend on
my support, guidance
friendship and love
every minute of every day
I love being your grandparent

When You Were Born,
I Wondered...

What will you see
in the future?
Will you see
beauty and goodness?
What will you hear
in the future?
Will you hear the sounds of
birds and songs?
What will you feel
in the future?
Will you feel
happy and fulfilled?

I hope that your life
will be completely
dominated
by passion and love
and that you will be able to
enjoy a life
of sensitivity
fairness
and accomplishment
in a world
that is at peace

I Have So Many Wishes for You

I wish for you to have
people to love
people in your life
who will care about you
   as much as I do
blue skies and clear days
exciting things to do

I wish for you to have
easy solutions to any problems
knowledge to make the right decisions
strength in your values
laughter and fun
goals to pursue
happiness in all that you do

I wish for you to have
beautiful experiences
each new day
as you follow
your dreams

At Six Weeks Old,
You Were Such a Mystery

What did your huge
eyes see
other than the
beauty from
everyone else's eyes?

What did your little
body feel
other than thirst and hunger
which were
immediately
alleviated by being fed?

What did your tiny
ears hear
other than music
and our soft words?

What did your
round mouth mean
with its coos
other than reacting
to the smiles
around you?

Your few needs were
met with calmness
and determination
You were so happy
and reassured
by the pure love
you saw and felt
every minute
you were awake
And we were so
blessed to share this
with you
We hoped it would be this way
for the rest of your life

I remember
rock, rock, rocking
all my love
into the beautiful miracle
that was you as a baby
hugging you so close
hoping my arms would
protect you from all
struggles
Rock, rock, rocking
as I gazed at this new life
that was you
kissing your little head
hoping that you would always be
as peaceful as you were then

I remember the feel
of your little breaths
against my heart when I held you as a baby
We would inhale together
in unison
Then we would exhale together
in song
I would hold you tightly
so you could feel the security of my arms
I would sing softly to you
so you would know the gentleness
     of my emotions
When your eyes opened
you would look at me for reassurance
Our bonding was boundless
I would kiss your soft cheek
as you peacefully fell asleep
absorbing the enormous love
surrounding you

My Thoughts on the Day
I Became a Grandparent...

My "baby"
has a baby
A pure innocent
beautiful new life
How could this be?
It seems like yesterday that
I was feeding
and kissing my child
whom I was holding
on my chest
And now
it's my child's baby
that I'm holding
and kissing
I'm almost in shock
as I look into the baby's eyes
and realize that my child
is a parent
It is such a miracle
such a reaffirmation
of all that's meaningful and spiritual
in life

That little smile
That little coo
Just so happy
with no burdens
no hatreds
Pure innocence
in an absolute
bubble of
love

You Were Always Such a Miracle

When you were a baby
how did you know
how to smile
so happily
so full of love
so genuinely
so innocently?
I would see this and
utter joy would emanate from my eyes
as I euphorically smiled back
Such a warm moment of love
shared

How did you know
how to cry
so painfully
so unhappily
so in need of something?
I would see this and
cradle your wet face in my hands
kissing you until all your tears were gone
Such a warm moment of comfort
shared

It was so miraculous
to see a little baby
who couldn't talk
who couldn't walk
look at me
with such a deep circle of emotions
which immediately flowed
through me

From the Start,
We Knew You'd Go Far

"Where is your nose?" I would ask
Yes, that is your
nose
"Where is your mouth?"
Yes, that is your
mouth
"Where is your hair?"
Yes, that is your
hair
"Where is your head?"
Yes, that is your
head
Learning every day
So curious
So alert
Just about ready for
college!

Words to Describe You
as a Baby...

Happy, smart, advanced, adorable
expressive, caring, sensitive, playful
exceptionally well behaved
and very well adjusted
Beautiful inside and out
A miracle of life
that radiates true joy

The Story of You

It is a story of
kindness
generosity
friendship and
love
A story
of a
child
who beautifully
demonstrates
a value of
compassion
that will last
a lifetime

I'll never forget
the first time I held you
You intently stared into my eyes
and I stared into yours
We were getting to know each other
And you were secure with my love
enveloping you like a cocoon
I didn't want to look elsewhere
because I was afraid you might feel that
    I had left you
I hoped that brief moment might
    contribute a little bit to
your confidence during your long life
    journey ahead
And then your little eyes closed
and you calmly went to sleep

I Am So Proud of You

I am so happy with the direction
that your life is taking you
You are unique and special
and I know that
your talents will give you
many paths to choose from
in the future
Always keep your many interests —
they will allow your mind
to remain energized
Always keep your positive outlook —
it will give you the strength to
accomplish great things
Always keep your determination —
it will give you the ability
to succeed in meeting your goals
Always keep your excitement
about whatever you do —
it will help you to have fun

Always keep your sense of humor —
it will allow you to
make mistakes and learn from them
Always keep your confidence —
it will allow you to take risks
and not be afraid of failure
Always keep your sensitivity —
it will help you to understand
and do something about
injustices in the world
Always remember that
I am more proud of you
than ever before

Beautiful
Grandchild

When you were a baby
you would turn your head from left to right
all by yourself
just like an athlete
You would scowl
in no uncertain terms
when you were not happy
and you would smile with glee
when you were
You made it very clear what you needed
Your eyes would tell everything

What a pleasurable wonder it has been
watching and helping you grow
to be a person of
compassion
creativity
strength
intelligence
beauty
independence
and a lot of joy
Never fear following your dreams
Never fear any obstacles that will come your way
Live your life with gusto
surrounded by continual
love

When You Were a Baby...

No crying
You would just quietly fall
asleep
for a short nap
on your favorite mat
with a toy mobile above
So peaceful and
content
In a trance
resting —
restoring your blessed
nature and health
I wondered what your
dreams were
and hoped you were recreating
the vast love
and enormous appreciation
of your life
that we all feel for you
My awake and
sleeping
dreams now
include the miracle
of you, my grandchild

There is no more
beautiful way to
spend my time
than having my grandchild
in my arms
with the look
of an angel
so pure and innocent
I gaze at your tired face
And outside in nature
a chorus of birds
sings a lullaby
as you fall
peacefully
asleep

Silly Rhymes Written to You Lovingly When You Were a Baby

You are so kind
And you have a very smart mind
You are always so sweet
You are a pure treat

You are my angel grandchild
You are like a strawberry bun
And you are so much fun
I like strawberry buns
But I like you more than a ton

You are a cuddly child
Your demeanor is so mild
But your jokes are so wild

Cotton Dog

Your quiet brown
    cotton dog
is not an oinking hog
It's your very own pet
who never goes to the vet
Cotton dog is your sleeping buddy
He is always clean and never muddy
He is very soft and cuddly
And is always happy and bubbly
Cotton dog shares your sleepy dream
What a sweet and loving team

You have big blue eyes
As bright as the clear sky
As delicious as an apple pie

Everyone loves you
Every single day
You are like a sunshine ray
In every way

"Who Do You Love?"

When you were small
I asked, "Who do you love?"
Your big eyes
expressed the love
that you understood
so well
And your big eyes
were so curious as
they looked at and
studied everything —
even a grain of
sand

And they laughed
when you were being funny
And they were so focused
when you did a mental task
And they squinted
when you said
"I want to nap!"
And they jumped for joy
when you fully woke up and saw us
    near your crib
It made our eyes fill with tears
realizing how important
we were and always will be
in your life
and how important you will always be in ours

I'm Glad to Be
Your Grandparent

There is a very special bond
between a grandparent
and grandchild
Both know that
neither is directly responsible for
the behavior of the other
yet the familial tie
is so strong
This results in a
relaxed relationship based on
love and giving into each other completely

Grandparents play games
with their grandchildren
that parents would never play
Grandparents take their grandchildren
to places that parents
would not think of
Grandparents give their grandchildren
an understanding of heritage
that parents cannot give
Grandparents and grandchildren
frolic in happiness in each other's presence
I am so glad to have
this wonderful, unique and
beautiful relationship
with you
my grandchild

You are such an outstanding person
and I hope nothing ever changes
your inner beauty
As you keep growing
remember always
to look at things the way you do now —
with sensitivity
honesty
compassion
and a touch of innocence
See the good in everything
and this will reflect back to you

Remember that people and situations
may not always be
as they appear
but if you remain true to yourself
it will be all right
When I look ahead
I see joy and fulfillment for you
    on every level
and I am so glad
because that is what every grandparent
wishes for a grandchild

Always Look for the Little Ray of Light

Look for the little light
Feel the little glow
Smell the little luster
If this infinitesimal light opens up
a tiny crack of the darkness
will guide you out
Embrace it with gratitude
kiss it
and touch it forever
Raise your arms and dance toward
the sky with
profound love

I hope that you always keep
your wonderful attitude
that whatever happens
in your life
happens for the best
I hope that you are always
truly happy and thankful
for whatever you have
and that you never care
about what you do not have
You are a very rare person
and you cannot imagine
how happy it makes me
to have you for my grandchild

In This Constantly Changing World, You Can Always Rely on Your Family

A family can give you
the freedom and backing
to go out in the world
and become a success
at whatever you want to do

A family is a structure built on love
from which you will
forever have support

A family is a relationship
that will grow through
good and bad times

A family is a commitment
to help each other and
to be as happy as possible in life

A family is a security that one
might not otherwise have
in the vast world

A family is thousands of
shared experiences

A family is inspirational

A family can give you the needed
confidence and happiness
to achieve great things
in the world

May You Always Know Love

Love is the strongest and
   most fulfilling emotion possible
It lets you share your goals, your desires
   your experiences
It lets you share your life with someone
It lets you be yourself with someone
   who will always support you
It lets you speak your innermost feelings
   to someone who understands you
It lets you feel tenderness and warmth —
   a wholeness that avoids loneliness
Love lets you feel complete

We must make the world
a place where
love dominates our hearts
nature sets the standard for beauty
simplicity and honesty are
the essence of our relationships
kindness guides our actions
and everyone respects one another

Two Special Memories
of You

Your grandfather was walking
confidently across the street
tightly holding you in his arms
You had one arm raised high
and your tiny head was above his
Your little cotton tie-dyed jacket
was blowing in the wind
There were big smiles on both of your faces
oblivious to the world
He protected and surrounded you with his love
and you were so happy and content
I looked at the two of you
and was so overwhelmed with emotion
Everything about our family
is a miracle
I love you all so much
and more each day

I am sitting on one end of our couch
Your grandfather is sitting on the other end
You are in the middle
hugging both of us
We are all singing to music
The love and
exhilaration within us
is as magnificent and mystical as the
biggest mountains
We are a part of the unitary family of
radiant nature

A Grandchild Is...

A kite flying through the trees
a tadpole turning into a frog
a dandelion in the wind
a mischievous smile
laughing eyes
a scrape on the knee
a wonder
an excitement, a burst of energy
an animation
a spirited breeze

A grandchild is
a rainbow bubble
a star glimmering in the sky
a rosebud after a storm
a caterpillar turning into a butterfly
hair flying in the wind
red cheeks that glisten in the sunshine
big daydream eyes
a wonder
a sweetness, a secret, an artist
a perception, a delight

A grandchild is love
and everything beautiful

Ever since you were born
you have been a bundle of
perpetual motion
Your energy is endless
Your mind is unbounded
You want to touch, smell, feel
    and do everything
You want to live life to the fullest

But don't forget
you are extraordinarily creative
and it is hard for creativity to flourish
unless there is a certain amount
of quietness and peace
So you will, at times, need to quell
your vigor
stop your movements
and let the perpetual motion of your mind
leap to new bounds
as you bask in the stillness of your
spirit and soul

Live in the Present and Make the Most of Every Day

Appreciate every moment
Dance
Sing
Play
Create
Love
Give
Help
Don't worry
Live in the present
Do not be a reflection of the rain
Be a reflection of the sun

If you make your own goals
if you adhere to your own values
if you choose your own kind of fun
you are living a life made by you
If other people are telling you what to do
or if you are copying other people's ways
or if you are acting out a certain lifestyle
    to impress people
you are living for other people rather than
    for yourself

People should not control you —
you must control your own life

Choose Your Friends
Carefully

It is easy to find a friend
when things are going well
and everyone can have fun together

It is easy to find a friend
when exciting things are happening
and everyone can look forward
    to them together

It is easy to find a friend
when the environment is attractive
and everyone can be happy together

But the friend that you find
who will be with you
when you are having problems
and your life is confused
is a hard friend to find

That rare person
is a friend
for life

As you keep growing and learning
striving and searching
it is very important
that you pursue your own interests
without anything holding you back
It will take time
to fully understand yourself
and to discover what you
want out of life
As you keep growing and learning
striving and searching
I know that the steps in your journey
will take you on the right path

This life is yours
Take the power
to choose what you want to do
and do it well
Take the power
to love what you want in life
and love honestly
Take the power
to walk in the forest
and be a part of nature
Take the power
to control your own life
No one else can do it for you
Take the power
to make your life
healthy
exciting
worthwhile
and very happy

Believe in Yourself
and Your Dreams

Dreams can come true if you take the time to
think about what you want in life...
Get to know yourself
Find out who you are
Choose your goals carefully
Be honest with yourself
Find many interests and pursue them
Find out what is important to you
Find out what you are good at
Don't be afraid to make mistakes
Work hard to achieve successes
When things are not going right
don't give up — just try harder
Find courage inside of you to remain strong
Give yourself freedom to try out new things
Don't be so set in your ways that you can't grow
Always act in an ethical way

Laugh and have a good time
Form relationships with people you respect
Treat others as you want them to treat you
Be honest with people
Accept the truth
Speak the truth
Open yourself up to love
Don't be afraid to love
Remain close to your family
Take part in the beauty of nature
Be appreciative of all that you have
Help those less fortunate than you
Try to make other lives happy
Work toward peace in the world
Live life to the fullest
Dreams can come true
and I hope that your dreams become a reality

Always Remember That You Have a Family Who Loves You

The love
of a family
is so
uplifting

The warmth
of a family
is so
comforting

The support
of a family
is so
reassuring

The attitude
of a family
toward each other
molds one's
attitude forever
toward the
world

A Family Holiday

Little grandchild
smiling and cuddling
talking, playing and hugging
Snowflakes on the windows
Dogs barking to go outside
Adults exchanging ideas, dreams and plans
Words of love
Eyes of love
Quietly reflecting
Outside the cold wind blowing
Inside we were very warm
wrapped in a blanket of love
A beautiful family holiday

I've been fortunate
to have been honored
in my life
But tucking you
my angel grandchild
into bed
is the most fulfilling honor
ever bestowed on me

My Little Angel

For the first seven days after you were born
you were the most peaceful, calm, happy baby
I had ever seen
Then you cried and cried
Your sounds
made us so sad
because we weren't able to help you
What was wrong?
What hurt?
I hoped whatever had made you so unhappy
would go away forever
and that in the future
your family's love and kisses would obliterate
any tears you might have

Once in a while
everyone needs
to know that they
are wanted
that they are important
that they are loved

If you ever feel
this need
I would like
to be the first one
to reassure you
that you are wanted
that you are important
and that I love you

I Will Always
Care About You
and Your Happiness

I want you to have a life of happiness
In order for you to have this
you must have many interests
and pursue them
You must have many goals
and work toward them
You must like your work
and always try to get better
You must consider yourself a success
by being proud of doing your best
You must have fun every day
You must listen to your own voice
and not be influenced by others

You must have someone who is
worthy of you to love
and to share your life
You must have peace
and not always expect perfection
You must have respect
for yourself and others
As I watch you grow up
I can see you are on the right path
and I am so proud of you
I will always care about you
and your happiness
I love you

How Will You Accept Life's Difficulties?

You can try to float
with the rip current
or drown in the waves
You can be sad yet accepting
You can dwell on unhappiness
You can give up
You can have rage
You can realize that life is uncertain
You can have hope for the future
You can appreciate love and joy

We are all at the mercy
of invisible forces that control
parts of our lives —
some beautiful
some tragic
We cannot alter these forces
so we have no choice
but to flow with them
and realize that we all
grow wiser and
become more sensitive and
are able to enjoy life more
after we go through
hard times

Take Time To...

Lean against a tree
and dream your world of dreams
Work hard at what you like to do
and try to overcome all obstacles
Laugh at your mistakes
and praise yourself for learning from them
Pick some flowers
and appreciate the beauty of nature
Be honest with people
and enjoy the good in them
Don't be afraid to show your emotions
Laughing and crying make you feel better

Love your friends and family with your
      entire being
They are the most important part of your life
Feel the calmness on a quiet sunny day
and plan what you want to accomplish in life
Find a rainbow
and live your
world of dreams

Only You Can Decide

So many choices
So many voices
People tugging a little
People pulling a little
Who to listen to
Which way to go
Everyone means well
The sounds are thunderous
The ideas are divergent
The only voice
that must matter
is the one that
resonates in your own heart
The only choice
that must matter
is the one that
you decide is right for you
Only you can decide what
the fabric of your life will be

We can't know
if it's this or that
in the future
We can only know what is
this moment

Explore Life
to the Fullest

Be a part of as many things as possible
Soak up everything
Look everywhere
Feed your spirit
Dance to the music you hear
Feel the plays you watch
Absorb the books you read
Be extremely curious
Touch nature
Help humanity
Celebrate love

Now is the time to
learn and grow
Now is the time to
explore and enjoy
the beauty of life

I Will Always Be Wishing for Your Success

What an incredible young person
you are growing up to be
I was proud of you when you were born
I was proud of you when you were
   a young child
Now as you continue
to grow in your own
unique, wonderful way
I am more proud of you
than ever before

Whatever happens in the future
I will always be wishing
for your happiness
and success
and at all times
I want you to know
that you have
my unconditional support
and love

I Feel So Fortunate to Have You for a Grandchild

I love your bright face
when we talk seriously about the world
I love your smile
when you laugh at the inconsistencies
     in the world
I love your eyes
when you are showing emotion
I love your mind
when you are discovering new ideas
and creating dreams to follow

I enjoy you so much and
I look forward to any time
we can spend together
Not only are you
    my adored grandchild
but you are also my friend

Grandchild, I Love You

To see you happy —
laughing and joking
smiling and content
striving toward goals of your own
accomplishing what you set out to do
having fun
capable of loving and being loved
is what I always wished for you

Today I thought about your
    precious face
and felt your excitement for life
and your genuine happiness
and I burst with pride
as I realized that my dreams
    for you have come true
What an extraordinary person
    you have become
and as you continue to grow
please remember always
how very much
I love you

About the Author

Susan Polis Schutz is an accomplished writer, poet, and documentary filmmaker. She is the author of many best-selling books of poetry illustrated by her husband, Stephen Schutz, including *To My Daughter with Love on the Important Things in Life*, which has sold over 1.8 million copies, and *To My Son with Love*, which has also enjoyed a wide audience. Susan's latest undertaking is creating documentary films that make a difference in people's lives with her production company, IronZeal Films. Her films have been shown on PBS stations throughout the country and include *The Misunderstood Epidemic: Depression*, which seeks to bring greater attention to this debilitating illness; *Over 90 and Loving It*, which features people in their 90s and 100s who are living extraordinary and passionate lives; and *Seeds of Resiliency*, which profiles twelve diverse people who have survived tragedies and challenges by having great hope and drawing on the resiliency inside themselves. Her newest film, *It's Just Anxiety?*, provides a very honest and insightful look at the various forms of anxiety and the ways people have overcome their anxiety.

Stephen Schutz has a PhD in physics from Princeton University and is an accomplished artist. In addition to designing and illustrating all of Susan's books, he is the genius behind bluemountain.com — the Internet greeting card service he created and cofounded with the help of his and Susan's elder son, Jared. He is also the founder of Starfall.com, an interactive website where children have fun while learning to read. In 2015, the Polis-Schutz family donated Starfall to the Starfall Education Foundation after supporting the project as a social enterprise for fifteen years.

Together, Susan and Stephen are the cofounders of Blue Mountain Arts, a popular publisher known for its distinctive greeting cards, gifts, and poetry books. Susan's poems and Stephen's artwork have been published on over 435 million greeting cards worldwide. Despite all their accomplishments, Susan and Stephen agree that their most fulfilling life experience has been being parents to their three children and grandparents to their two grandchildren.